Sports Illustrated KIDS

FOR THE RECORD

THE ULTIMATE COLLECTION OF PRO FOOTBALL RECORDS

BY SHANE FREDERICK

CAPSTONE PRESS
a capstone imprint

Sports Illustrated Kids For the Record is published by Capstone Press,
1710 Roe Crest Drive, North Mankato, Minnesota 56003.
www.capstonepub.com

Library of Congress Cataloging-in-Publication Data
Frederick, Shane.
   The ultimate collection of pro football records / by Shane Frederick.
   p. cm.—(Sports Illustrated Kids. For the Record)
   Includes bibliographical references and index.
   ISBN 978-1-4296-8578-8 (library binding)
   ISBN 978-1-4296-9432-2 (paperback)
   1. Football—Records—United States—Juvenile literature. I. Title.
GV955.F74 2013
796.332'64—dc23   2012006162

Editorial Credits
Anthony Wacholtz, editor; Ted Williams, designer; Eric Gohl, media researcher;
      Eric Manske, production specialist

Photo Credits
BigStockPhoto.com: RTImages, back cover (football); Corbis: Bettmann, 8t, 27b, 38t;
Library of Congress: 59t; Newscom: Icon Sports Media, 29b, UPI/Frederick Breedon IV,
24t; Shutterstock: Kim Reinick, cover, Photoroller, back cover (field); Sports Illustrated: Al
Tielemans, 22b, 30t, 37l, 39b, 43b, 48t, 53t, 53b, 54t, Andy Hayt, 3, 8b, 9b, 13b, 21b, 25t,
28b, 32t, 41t, 43t, Bill Frakes, 2t, 2m, 9t, 14b, 27t, 28t, 54b, 61b, Bob Rosato, 7t, 18b, 23t,
26b, 29t, 33, 34b, 37r, 39tl, 60, Damian Strohmeyer, 7b, 16b, 19b, 23b, 36, 38b, 39tr, 45t,
51b, 58tr, 61t, David E. Klutho, 11b, 16t, 18t, Heinz Kluetmeier, 2b, 25b, 27m, 45b, 46l, Hy
Peskin, 52b, John Biever, 6, 17b, 30b, 31, 32b, 41b, 50b, 56, 58br, John Iacono, 10t, 12t, 13t,
15b, 19t, 20, 22t, 42, 44t, 47t, 48b, 49b, 55t, 55b, 59b, John W. McDonough, 10b, 47b, Lane
Stewart, 35b, Manny Millan, 40, Peter Read Miller, 11t, 14t, 15t, 17t, 21t, 24b, 49tl, 51t, 52t,
57, 58l, Robert Beck, 4–5, 34t, Simon Bruty, 26t, 50t, Walter Iooss Jr., 12b, 35t, 44b, 46r,
49tr

Design Elements
BigStockPhoto.com: RTImages; Shutterstock: fmua, Photoroller, ssuaphotos

Printed in the United States of America in North Mankato, Minnesota.
042012   006682CGF12

TABLE OF CONTENTS

RECORDS OF THE GRIDIRON

San Francisco 49ers quarterback Steve Young dropped back to pass. He found his target and launched the ball nearly 40 yards to the end zone. Receiver Jerry Rice leaped up, grabbed the ball, and fell to the turf between three Los Angeles Raiders defensive backs for a touchdown. Teammates hugged Rice and lifted him onto their shoulders. It was no ordinary touchdown. It was a record breaker.

Rice's touchdown was the third of that 1994 Monday Night Football game and the 127th of his career. Before that catch, no player in the history of the NFL had scored that many touchdowns. The previous record of 126 was set almost 30 years earlier by Jim Brown, a running back for the Cleveland Browns.

Setting a record is a historic event. It establishes a player as one of the greats of the sport.

RECORD FACT Records for pro football have been kept since 1920, when the league was known as the American Professional Football Association. Two years later the league changed its name to the National Football League.

*All stats are through the 2011 NFL season.

It's a measuring stick for young and future players.

Jerry Rice set the NFL's career touchdown record that night. He ended his career with 208 touchdowns, which still stands as a record. But some players have come close to claiming the top spot. In fact, Brown's old record now ranks 10th on the all-time list.

Emmitt Smith and Terrell Owens couldn't catch Rice.

Who will be the next player to get close? Larry Fitzgerald? Arian Foster? Calvin Johnson?

What do you think is the greatest record in NFL history? Is it Rice's touchdown mark? Maybe it's Brett Favre's playing streak, the New England Patriots' 2007 point total, or the Chicago Bears' 73-0 championship-game win in 1940. Not sure? Read on—you're bound to find your favorite!

CHAPTER 1

PLAYER RECORDS

For 20 years Miami Dolphins great Dan Marino held the NFL record for passing touchdowns in a single season. He threw 48 scoring passes in 1984. The number amazed fans. It crushed the league's previous record of 36 from 1961. Some thought it was a record that would never be broken.

But in 2004 Peyton Manning of the Indianapolis Colts set a new record with 49 touchdown passes. The record didn't stay with Manning long. The New England Patriots' Tom Brady tossed 50 in 2007.

Will Brady hold that record for 20 years? Or will Aaron Rodgers or Philip Rivers hit 51? Will anyone top Eric Dickerson's 2,105 single-season rushing yards? Or Brandon Marshall's 21 pass receptions in a single game?

When it comes to individual players, records can define greatness, whether it's over a career, a season, or even one game. Even making it into the top 10 of these categories is a great accomplishment.

▲ Peyton Manning signed with the Denver Broncos after the 2011 season.

PASSING TOUCHDOWNS

▼ Brett Favre

CAREER ||||||||||||||||||||||||||||||||||||||||||||||||||

1.	Brett Favre	508	Falcons/Packers/Jets/Vikings	1991–2010
2.	Dan Marino	420	Dolphins	1983–1999
3.	Peyton Manning	399	Colts	1998–2011*
4.	Fran Tarkenton	342	Vikings/Giants	1961–1978
5.	Tom Brady	300	Patriots	2000–2011*
	John Elway	300	Broncos	1983–1998
7.	Warren Moon	291	Oilers/Vikings/Seahawks/Chiefs	1984–2000
8.	Johnny Unitas	290	Colts/Chargers	1956–1973
9.	Drew Brees	281	Chargers/Saints	2001–2011*
10.	Vinny Testaverde	275	Buccaneers/Browns/Ravens/Jets/Cowboys/Patriots/Panthers	1987–2007

*active player

SINGLE SEASON |||||||||||||||||||||||||||||||||||||||||

1.	Tom Brady	50	Patriots	2007
2.	Peyton Manning	49	Colts	2004
3.	Dan Marino	48	Dolphins	1984
4.	Drew Brees	46	Saints	2011
5.	Aaron Rodgers	45	Packers	2011
6.	Dan Marino	44	Dolphins	1986
7.	Matthew Stafford	41	Lions	2011
	Kurt Warner	41	Rams	1999
9.	Tom Brady	39	Patriots	2011
	Daunte Culpepper	39	Vikings	2004
	Brett Favre	39	Packers	1996

▲ Tom Brady

🏈 PASSING TOUCHDOWNS

▼ Sid Luckman

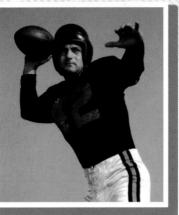

SINGLE GAME ||||||||||||||||||||||||||||||||||||

1.	George Blanda	7	Oilers	Nov. 19, 1961
	Adrian Burk	7	Eagles	Oct. 17, 1954
	Joe Kapp	7	Vikings	Sept. 28, 1969
	Sid Luckman	7	Bears	Nov. 14, 1943
	Y.A. Tittle	7	Giants	Oct. 28, 1962
2.	Many players tied with	6		

🏈 PASSING YARDS

CAREER ||||||||||||||||||||||||||||||||||||

1.	Brett Favre	71,838	Falcons/Packers/Jets/Vikings	1991–2010
2.	Dan Marino	61,361	Dolphins	1983–1999
3.	Peyton Manning	54,828	Colts	1998–2011*
4.	John Elway	51,475	Broncos	1983–1998
5.	Warren Moon	49,325	Oilers/Vikings/Seahawks/Chiefs	1984–2000
6.	Fran Tarkenton	47,003	Vikings/Giants	1961–1978
7.	Vinny Testaverde	46,233	Buccaneers/Browns/Ravens/Jets/Cowboys/Patriots/Panthers	1987–2007
8.	Drew Bledsoe	44,611	Patriots/Bills/Cowboys	1993–2006
9.	Dan Fouts	43,040	Chargers	1973–1987
10.	Kerry Collins	40,922	Panthers/Saints/Giants/Raiders/Titans/Colts	1995–2011

*active player

▲ John Elway

 Before he played in the NFL, Warren Moon spent six seasons in the Canadian Football League. He led the Edmonton Eskimos to five straight Grey Cup championship victories.

During his CFL career, he compiled 21,228 passing yards and 144 touchdowns. Add those to his NFL numbers, and he'd rank second all-time in both categories.

 ## PASSING YARDS

SINGLE SEASON			
1. Drew Brees	5,476	Saints	2011
2. Tom Brady	5,235	Patriots	2011
3. Dan Marino	5,084	Dolphins	1984
4. Drew Brees	5,069	Saints	2008
5. Matthew Stafford	5,038	Lions	2011
6. Eli Manning	4,933	Giants	2011
7. Kurt Warner	4,830	Rams	2001
8. Tom Brady	4,806	Patriots	2007
9. Dan Fouts	4,802	Chargers	1981
10. Matt Schaub	4,770	Texans	2009

▲ Dan Marino

SINGLE GAME			
1. Norm Van Brocklin	554	Rams	Sept. 28, 1951
2. Warren Moon	527	Oilers	Dec. 16, 1990
3. Boomer Esiason	522	Cardinals	Nov. 10, 1996
4. Dan Marino	521	Dolphins	Oct. 23, 1988
5. Matthew Stafford	520	Lions	Jan. 1, 2012
6. Tom Brady	517	Patriots	Sept. 12, 2011
7. Phil Simms	513	Giants	Oct. 31, 1985
8. Drew Brees	510	Saints	Nov. 19, 2006
9. Vince Ferragamo	509	Rams	Dec. 26, 1982
10. Y.A. Tittle	505	Giants	Oct. 28, 1962

▲ Phil Simms

COMPLETIONS

CARERR ||||||||||||||||||||||||||||||||||||||||||||

1.	Brett Favre	6,300	Falcons/Packers/Jets/Vikings	1991–2010
2.	Dan Marino	4,967	Dolphins	1983–1999
3.	Peyton Manning	4,682	Colts	1998–2011*
4.	John Elway	4,123	Broncos	1983–1998
5.	Warren Moon	3,988	Oilers/Vikings/Seahawks/Chiefs	1984–2000
6.	Drew Bledsoe	3,839	Patriots/Bills/Cowboys	1993–2006
7.	Vinny Testaverde	3,787	Buccaneers/Browns/Ravens/Jets/Cowboys/Patriots/Panthers	1987–2007
8.	Fran Tarkenton	3,686	Vikings/Giants	1961–1978
9.	Drew Brees	3,494	Saints	2001–2011*
10.	Kerry Collins	3,487	Panthers/Saints/Giants/Raiders/Titans/Colts	1995–2011

*active player

SINGLE SEASON ||||||||||||||||||||||||||||||||||||||||||

1.	Drew Brees	468	Saints	2011
2.	Peyton Manning	450	Colts	2010
3.	Drew Brees	448	Saints	2010
4.	Drew Brees	440	Saints	2007
5.	Matthew Stafford	421	Lions	2011
6.	Rich Gannon	418	Raiders	2002
7.	Drew Brees	413	Saints	2008
8.	Warren Moon	404	Oilers	1991
9.	Tom Brady	401	Patriots	2011
	Kurt Warner	401	Cardinals	2008

▲ Drew Brees

COMPLETIONS

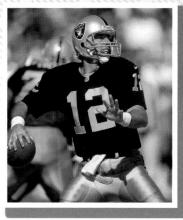

SINGLE GAME

1.	Drew Bledsoe	45	Patriots	Nov. 13, 1994
2.	Rich Gannon	43	Raiders	Sept. 15, 2002
3.	Vinny Testaverde	42	Jets	Dec. 6, 1998
	Richard Todd	42	Jets	Sept. 21, 1980
5.	Warren Moon	41	Oilers	Nov. 10, 1991
	Tony Romo	41	Cowboys	Dec. 6, 2009
7.	Many players tied with	40		

QUARTERBACK RATING

A complex formula is used to determine how well a quarterback is playing. Called the quarterback rating, the formula takes into account completions, attempts, passing yards, touchdowns, and interceptions. In 2011 the Packers' Aaron Rodgers set the single-season quarterback rating record with 122.5. The Colts' Peyton Manning held the old mark of 121.1, set in 2004.

▼ Aaron Rodgers

INTERCEPTIONS

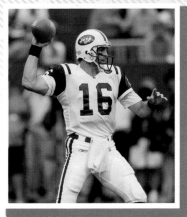

CARERE ||||||||||||||||||||||||||||||||||||||||||

1.	Brett Favre	336	Falcons/Packers/Jets/Vikings	1991–2010
2.	George Blanda	277	Bears/Colts/Oilers/Raiders	1949–1975
3.	John Hadl	268	Chargers/Rams/Packers/Oilers	1962–1977
4.	Vinny Testaverde	267	Buccaneers/Browns/Ravens/Jets/Cowboys/Patriots/Panthers	1987–2007
5.	Fran Tarkenton	266	Vikings/Giants	1961–1978
6.	Norm Snead	257	Redskins/Eagles/Vikings/Giants/49ers	1961–1976
7.	Johnny Unitas	253	Colts/Chargers	1956–1973
8.	Dan Marino	252	Dolphins	1983–1999
9.	Y.A. Tittle	248	Colts/49ers/Giants	1948–1964
10.	Jim Hart	247	Cardinals/Redskins	1966–1984

SINGLE SEASON ||||||||||||||||||||||||||||||||||||||

1.	George Blanda	42	Oilers	1962
2.	Vinny Testaverde	35	Buccaneers	1988
3.	Frank Tripucka	34	Broncos	1960
4.	John Hadl	32	Chargers	1968
	Fran Tarkenton	32	Vikings	1978
6.	Sid Luckman	31	Bears	1947
7.	Five players tied with	30		

▲ **Fran Tarkenton**

RECORD FACT In 1978 the NFL went from a 14-game schedule to a 16-game schedule. Adding two games had an impact on many records. Players had two extra games to chase single-season records. Those extra games added to players' career numbers too.

RUSHING

🏈 RUSHING YARDS

CAREER ||||||||||||||||||||||||||||||||||||||||||||||||||

1.	Emmitt Smith	18,355	Cowboys/Cardinals	1990–2004
2.	Walter Payton	16,726	Bears	1975–1987
3.	Barry Sanders	15,269	Lions	1989–1998
4.	Curtis Martin	14,101	Patriots/Jets	1995–2005
5.	LaDainian Tomlinson	13,684	Chargers/Jets	2001–2011*
6.	Jerome Bettis	13,662	Rams/Steelers	1993–2005
7.	Eric Dickerson	13,259	Rams/Colts/Raiders/Falcons	1983–1993
8.	Tony Dorsett	12,739	Cowboys/Broncos	1977–1988
9.	Jim Brown	12,312	Browns	1957–1965
10.	Marshall Faulk	12,279	Colts/Rams	1994–2005

*active player

▲ Walter Payton

SINGLE SEASON |||||||||||||||||||||||||||||||||||||||||||

1.	Eric Dickerson	2,105	Rams	1984
2.	Jamal Lewis	2,066	Ravens	2003
3.	Barry Sanders	2,053	Lions	1997
4.	Terrell Davis	2,008	Broncos	1998
5.	Chris Johnson	2,006	Titans	2009
6.	O.J. Simpson	2,003	Bills	1973
7.	Earl Campbell	1,934	Oilers	1980
8.	Ahman Green	1,883	Packers	2003
	Barry Sanders	1,883	Lions	1993
10.	Shaun Alexander	1,880	Seahawks	2005

▲ Eric Dickerson

⬤ RUSHING YARDS

SINGLE GAME

1.	Adrian Peterson	296	Vikings	Nov. 4, 2007
2.	Jamal Lewis	295	Ravens	Sept. 14, 2003
3.	Jerome Harrison	286	Browns	Dec. 20, 2009
4.	Corey Dillon	278	Bengals	Oct. 22, 2000
5.	Walter Payton	275	Bears	Nov. 20, 1977
6.	O.J. Simpson	273	Bills	Nov. 25, 1976
7.	Shaun Alexander	266	Seahawks	Nov. 11, 2001
8.	Jamaal Charles	259	Chiefs	Jan. 3, 2010
9.	DeMarco Murray	253	Cowboys	Oct. 23, 2011
10.	Mike Anderson	251	Broncos	Dec. 3, 2000

⬤ RUSHING TOUCHDOWNS

CAREER

1.	Emmitt Smith	164	Cowboys/Cardinals	1990–2004
2.	LaDainian Tomlinson	145	Chargers/Jets	2001–2011*
3.	Marcus Allen	123	Raiders/Chiefs	1982–1997
4.	Walter Payton	110	Bears	1975–1987
5.	Jim Brown	106	Browns	1957–1965
6.	John Riggins	104	Jets/Redskins	1971–1985
7.	Shaun Alexander	100	Seahawks/Redskins	2000–2008
	Marshall Faulk	100	Colts/Rams	1994–2005
9.	Barry Sanders	99	Lions	1989–1998
10.	Jerome Bettis	91	Rams/Steelers	1993–2005
	Franco Harris	91	Steelers/Seahawks	1972–1984

▲ Emmitt Smith

*active player

RUSHING TOUCHDOWNS

SINGLE SEASON ||||||||||||||||||||||||||||||||||||

1.	LaDainian Tomlinson	28	Chargers	2006
2.	Shaun Alexander	27	Seahawks	2005
	Priest Holmes	27	Chiefs	2003
4.	Emmitt Smith	26	Cowboys	1995
5.	John Riggins	24	Redskins	1983
6.	Terry Allen	21	Redskins	1996
	Terrell Davis	21	Broncos	1998
	Priest Holmes	21	Chiefs	2002
	Joe Morris	21	Giants	1985
	Emmitt Smith	21	Cowboys	1994

RECORD FACT Ernie Nevers holds the record for rushing touchdowns in one game. He scored six times for the Chicago Cardinals on November 28, 1929.

LONGEST RUN |||||||||||||||||||||||||||||||||||||||||

1.	Tony Dorsett	99 yards	Cowboys	Jan. 3, 1983
2.	Ahman Green	98 yards	Packers	Dec. 28, 2003
3.	Bob Gage	97 yards	Steelers	Dec. 4, 1949
	Andy Uram	97 yards	Packers	Oct. 8, 1939
5.	Corey Dillon	96 yards	Bengals	Oct. 28, 2001
	Garrison Hearst	96 yards	49ers	Sept. 6, 1998
	Bob Hoernschemeyer	96 yards	Lions	Nov. 23, 1950
	Jim Spavital	96 yards	Colts	Nov. 5, 1950
9.	Tiki Barber	95 yards	Giants	Dec. 31, 2005
	Chester Taylor	95 yards	Vikings	Oct. 22, 2006

▲ Tony Dorsett

RECEPTIONS

▼ Tony Gonzalez

CAREER

1.	Jerry Rice	1,549	49ers/Raiders/Seahawks	1985–2004
2.	Tony Gonzalez	1,149	Chiefs/Falcons	1997–2011*
3.	Marvin Harrison	1,102	Colts	1996–2008
4.	Cris Carter	1,101	Eagles/Vikings/Dolphins	1987–2002
5.	Tim Brown	1,094	Raiders/Buccaneers	1988–2004
6.	Terrell Owens	1,078	49ers/Eagles/Cowboys/Bills/Bengals	1996–2010
7.	Isaac Bruce	1,024	Rams/49ers	1994–2009
8.	Hines Ward	1,000	Steelers	1998–2011
9.	Randy Moss	954	Vikings/Raiders/Patriots/Titans	1998–2010
10.	Andre Reed	951	Bills/Redskins	1985–2000

*active player

SINGLE SEASON

1.	Marvin Harrison	143	Colts	2002
2.	Herman Moore	123	Lions	1995
	Wes Welker	123	Patriots	2009
4.	Cris Carter	122	Vikings	1994
	Cris Carter	122	Vikings	1995
	Jerry Rice	122	49ers	1995
	Wes Welker	122	Patriots	2011
8.	Isaac Bruce	119	Rams	1995
9.	Torry Holt	117	Rams	2003
10.	Jimmy Smith	116	Jaguars	1999

▲ Wes Welker

RECEPTIONS

▼ Brandon Marshall

SINGLE GAME

1.	Brandon Marshall	21	Broncos	Dec. 13, 2009
2.	Terrell Owens	20	49ers	Dec. 17, 2000
3.	Tom Fears	18	Rams	Dec. 3, 1950
	Brandon Marshall	18	Broncos	Sept. 14, 2008
5.	Clark Gaines	17	Jets	Sept. 21, 1980
6.	Troy Brown	16	Patriots	Sept. 22, 2002
	Keenan McCardell	16	Jaguars	Oct. 20, 1996
	Jerry Rice	16	49ers	Nov. 20, 1994
	Sonny Randle	16	Cardinals	Nov. 4, 1962
	Wes Welker	16	Patriots	Sept. 25, 2011

RECEIVING YARDS

CAREER

1.	Jerry Rice	22,895	49ers/Raiders/Seahawks	1985–2004
2.	Terrell Owens	15,934	49ers/Eagles/Cowboys/Bills/Bengals	1996–2010
3.	Isaac Bruce	15,208	Rams/49ers	1994–2009
4.	Tim Brown	14,934	Raiders/Buccaneers	1988–2004
5.	Randy Moss	14,858	Vikings/Raiders/Patriots/Titans	1998–2010
6.	Marvin Harrison	14,580	Colts	1996–2008
7.	James Lofton	14,004	Packers/Raiders/Bills/Rams/Eagles	1978–1993
8.	Cris Carter	13,899	Eagles/Vikings/Dolphins	1987–2002
9.	Henry Ellard	13,777	Rams/Redskins/Patriots	1983–1998
10.	Torry Holt	13,382	Rams/Jaguars	1999–2009

▲ Terrell Owens

RECEIVING YARDS

SINGLE SEASON

1.	Jerry Rice	1,848	49ers	1995
2.	Isaac Bruce	1,781	Rams	1995
3.	Charley Hennigan	1,746	Oilers	1961
4.	Marvin Harrison	1,722	Colts	2002
5.	Torry Holt	1,696	Rams	2003
6.	Herman Moore	1,686	Lions	1995
7.	Calvin Johnson	1,681	Lions	2011
8.	Marvin Harrison	1,663	Colts	1999
9.	Jimmy Smith	1,636	Jaguars	1999
10.	Torry Holt	1,635	Rams	2000

SINGLE GAME

1.	Flipper Anderson	336	Rams	Nov. 26, 1989
2.	Stephone Paige	309	Chiefs	Dec. 22, 1985
3.	Jim Benton	303	Rams	Nov. 22, 1945
4.	Cloyce Box	302	Lions	Dec. 3, 1950
5.	Jimmy Smith	291	Jaguars	Sept. 10, 2000
6.	Jerry Rice	289	49ers	Dec. 18, 1995
7.	John Taylor	286	49ers	Dec. 11, 1989
8.	Terrell Owens	283	49ers	Dec. 17, 2000
9.	Charley Hennigan	272	Oilers	Oct. 13, 1961
10.	Del Shofner	269	Giants	Oct. 28, 1962

▲ Jimmy Smith

RECORD FACT Fifteen players in NFL history have caught passes for 99 yards. The first was Andy Farkas of the Redskins in 1939. It happened twice in 2011, once by Wes Welker of the Patriots and another by Victor Cruz of the Giants.

Nine other players have 98-yard receptions. In 1972 the Cardinals' Jim Hart threw a 98-yard pass to Bobby Moore, but he didn't score a touchdown. Moore went from the Cardinals' 1-yard line to the Rams' 1-yard line.

🏈 RECEIVING TOUCHDOWNS

CAREER

1.	Jerry Rice	197	49ers/Raiders/Seahawks	1985–2004
2.	Randy Moss	153	Vikings/Raiders/Patriots/Titans	1998–2010
	Terrell Owens	153	49ers/Eagles/Cowboys/Bills/Bengals	1996–2010
4.	Cris Carter	130	Eagles/Vikings/Dolphins	1987–2002
5.	Marvin Harrison	128	Colts	1996–2008
6.	Tim Brown	100	Raiders/Buccaneers	1988–2004
	Steve Largent	100	Seahawks	1976–1989
8.	Don Hutson	99	Packers	1935–1945
9.	Tony Gonzalez	95	Chiefs/Falcons	1997–2011*
10.	Isaac Bruce	91	Rams/49ers	1994–2009

SINGLE SEASON

1.	Randy Moss	23	Patriots	2007
2.	Jerry Rice	22	49ers	1987
3.	Mark Clayton	18	Dolphins	1984
	Sterling Sharpe	18	Packers	1994
5.	Cris Carter	17	Vikings	1995
	Bill Groman	17	Oilers	1961
	Rob Gronkowski	17	Patriots	2011
	Elroy Hirsch	17	Rams	1951
	Don Hutson	17	Packers	1942
	Randy Moss	17	Vikings	1998
	Randy Moss	17	Vikings	2003
	Carl Pickens	17	Bengals	1995
	Jerry Rice	17	49ers	1989

▲ Randy Moss

🏈 POINTS

▼ John Carney

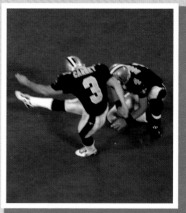

CAREER ||||||||||||||||||||||||||||||||||||||||||||||

1.	**Morten Andersen, K**	2,544	Saints/Falcons/ Giants/Chiefs/ Vikings	1982–2007
2.	**Gary Anderson, K**	2,434	Steelers/Eagles/ 49ers/Vikings/ Titans	1982–2004
3.	**John Carney, K**	2,062	Buccaneers/ Chargers/Rams/ Saints/Chiefs/ Jaguars/Giants	1988–2010
4.	**Jason Hanson, K**	2,016	Lions	1992–2011*
5.	**Matt Stover, K**	2,004	Browns/Ravens/ Colts	1991–2009
6.	**George Blanda, QB/K/LB**	2,002	Colts/Bears/ Oilers/Raiders	1949–1975
7.	**Jason Elam, K**	1,983	Broncos/Falcons	1993–2009
8.	**John Kasay, K**	1,970	Seahawks/ Panthers/Saints	1991–2011*
9.	**Adam Vinatieri, K**	1,752	Patriots/Colts	1996–2011*
10.	**Norm Johnson, K**	1,736	Seahawks/ Falcons/ Steelers/Eagles	1982–1999

*active player

RECORD FACT Ernie Nevers, Dub Jones, and Gale Sayers are the only players to score six touchdowns in one game. Nevers' scores all came on the ground. He added four PATs (points after touchdown) for 40 total points. Jones ran for four scores and caught two touchdown passes. Sayers had four rushing, one receiving, and one punt return for a touchdown. Paul Hornung once scored 33 points in one game with four touchdowns, six PATs, and one field goal.

POINTS

SINGLE SEASON ||||||||||||||||||||||||||||||||||||||

1.	LaDainian Tomlinson, RB	186	Chargers	2006
2.	Paul Hornung, RB/K	176	Packers	1960
3.	Shaun Alexander, RB	168	Seahawks	2005
4.	David Akers, K	166	49ers	2011
5.	Gary Anderson, K	164	Vikings	1998
6.	Jeff Wilkins, K	163	Rams	2003
7.	Priest Holmes, RB	162	Chiefs	2003
8.	Mark Moseley, K	161	Redskins	1983
9.	Marshall Faulk, RB	160	Rams	2000
10.	Mike Vanderjagt, K	157	Colts	2003

TOUCHDOWNS

CAREER ||||||||||||||||||||||||||||||||||||||

1.	Jerry Rice, WR	208	49ers/Raiders/Seahawks	1985–2004
2.	Emmitt Smith, RB	175	Cowboys/Cardinals	1990–2004
3.	LaDainian Tomlinson, RB	162	Chargers/Jets	2001–2011*
4.	Terrell Owens, WR	156	49ers/Eagles/Cowboys/Bills/Bengals	1996–2010
5.	Randy Moss, WR	154	Vikings/Raiders/Patriots/Titans	1998–2010*
6.	Marcus Allen, RB	145	Raiders/Chiefs	1982–1997
7.	Marshall Faulk, RB	136	Colts/Rams	1994–2005
8.	Cris Carter, WR	131	Eagles/Vikings/Dolphins	1987–2002
9.	Marvin Harrison, WR	128	Colts	1996–2008
10.	Jim Brown, RB	126	Browns	1957–1965

*active player

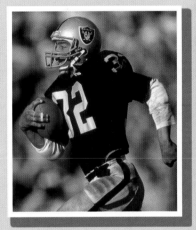

▲ Marcus Allen

TOUCHDOWNS

SINGLE SEASON

1.	LaDainian Tomlinson, RB	31	Chargers	2006
2.	Shaun Alexander, RB	28	Seahawks	2005
3.	Priest Holmes, RB	27	Chiefs	2003
4.	Marshall Faulk, RB	26	Rams	2000
5.	Emmitt Smith, RB	25	Cowboys	1995
6.	Priest Holmes, RB	24	Chiefs	2002
	John Riggins, RB	24	Redskins	1983
8.	Terrell Davis, RB	23	Broncos	1998
	Randy Moss, WR	23	Patriots	2007
	Jerry Rice, WR	23	49ers	1987
	O.J. Simpson, RB	23	Bills	1975

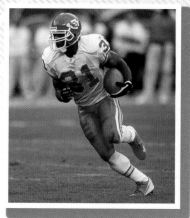

DEFENSIVE SCORERS

▼ Deion Sanders

The career record holder for non-offensive touchdowns is Deion Sanders. He scored 19 times for five teams from 1989 to 2005. Those scores came on nine interceptions, six punt returns, three kickoff returns, and one fumble recovery. Although he was mostly a defensive back, he also caught three passes for touchdowns in his career. The Chicago Bears' Devin Hester holds the single-season record for non-offensive touchdowns. He scored six non-offensive touchdowns in both 2006 and 2007.

KICKING

FIELD GOALS

CAREER

1.	Morten Andersen	565	Saints/Falcons/Giants/Chiefs/Vikings	1982–2007
2.	Gary Anderson	538	Steelers/Eagles/49ers/Vikings/Titans	1982–2004
3.	John Carney	478	Buccaneers/Rams/Chargers/Saints/Jaguars/Chiefs/Giants	1988–2010
4.	Matt Stover	471	Browns/Ravens/Colts	1991–2009
5.	Jason Hanson	463	Lions	1992–2011*
6.	John Kasay	461	Seahawks/Panthers/Saints	1991–2011*
7.	Jason Elam	436	Broncos/Falcons	1993–2009
8.	Adam Vinatieri	387	Patriots/Colts	1996–2011*
9.	Nick Lowery	383	Patriots/Chiefs/Jets	1978–1996
10.	Jan Stenerud	373	Chiefs/Packers/Vikings	1967–1985

*active player

SINGLE SEASON

1.	David Akers	44	49ers	2011
2.	Neil Rackers	40	Cardinals	2005
3.	Olindo Mare	39	Dolphins	1999
	Jeff Wilkins	39	Rams	2003
5.	John Kasay	37	Panthers	1996
	Mike Vanderjagt	37	Colts	2003
7.	Cary Blanchard	36	Colts	1996
	Stephen Gostkowski	36	Patriots	2008
	Al Del Greco	36	Titans	1998
10.	Many players tied with	35		

▲ Stephen Gostkowski

⬤ FIELD GOALS

SINGLE GAME ||||||||||||||||||||||||||||||||||

1.	**Rob Bironas**	8	Titans	Oct. 21, 2007
2.	**Jim Bakken**	7	Cardinals	Sept. 24, 1967
	Chris Boniol	7	Cowboys	Nov. 18, 1996
	Billy Cundiff	7	Cowboys	Sept. 15, 2003
	Shayne Graham	7	Bengals	Nov. 11, 2007
	Rich Karlis	7	Vikings	Nov. 5, 1989

LEGGING IT OUT

The longest field goal in NFL history is 63 yards. It has happened three times. The New Orleans Saints' Tom Dempsey accomplished the feat November 8, 1970. The others were kicked in the thin air of Denver, Colorado. The Broncos' Jason Elam made one October 25, 1998. The Oakland Raiders' Sebastian Janikowski did it against the Broncos on September 12, 2011. Janikowski also holds the record for the longest field goal try, once lining up for a 76-yarder!

▲ Sebastian Janikowski

INTERCEPTIONS

CAREER

1.	Paul Krause	81	Redskins/Vikings	1964–1979
2.	Emlen Tunnell	79	Giants/Packers	1948–1961
3.	Rod Woodson	71	Steelers/49ers/ Ravens/Raiders	1987–2003
4.	Dick "Night Train" Lane	68	Rams/Cardinals/ Lions	1952–1965
5.	Ken Riley	65	Bengals	1969–1983
6.	Ronnie Lott	63	49ers/Raiders/Jets	1981–1994
	Darren Sharper	63	Packers/Vikings/ Saints	1997–2010
8.	Dave Brown	62	Steelers/Seahawks/ Packers	1975–1989
	Dick LeBeau	62	Lions	1959–1972
10.	Emmitt Thomas	58	Chiefs	1966–1978

SINGLE SEASON

1.	Dick "Night Train" Lane	14	Rams	1952
2.	Lester Hayes	13	Raiders	1980
	Spec Sanders	13	Yankees	1950
	Dan Sandifer	13	Redskins	1948
5.	Many players tied with	12		

▲ **Lester Hayes**

RECORD FACT Eighteen players in NFL history have intercepted four passes in one game.

INTERCEPTIONS

CAREER INTERCEPTION RETURNS FOR TOUCHDOWNS | | |

1.	Rod Woodson	12	Steelers/49ers/Ravens/Raiders	1987–2003
2.	Darren Sharper	11	Packers/Vikings/Saints	1997–2010
	Charles Woodson	11	Raiders/Packers	1998–2011*
4.	Ken Houston	9	Oilers/Redskins	1967–1980
	Deion Sanders	9	Falcons/49ers/Cowboys/Redskins/Ravens	1989–2005
	Aeneas Williams	9	Cardinals/Rams	1991–2004
7.	Eric Allen	8	Eagles/Saints/Raiders	1988–2001
8.	Six players tied with	7		

*active player

▲ Ed Reed

RECORD FACTS Three players share the single-season record for interception returns for touchdowns with four each. They are the Houston Oilers' Ken Houston (1971), the Kansas City Chiefs' Jim Kearney (1972), and the Philadelphia Eagles' Eric Allen (1993).

There have been 31 interception returns of 100 yards or more. Baltimore Ravens All-Pro defensive back Ed Reed owns the two longest returns, taking one 107 yards and another 106 yards.

DEFENSIVE FUMBLE RECOVERIES

▼ Jason Taylor

CAREER

1.	Jim Marshall	29	Browns/Vikings	1961–1979
2.	Rickey Jackson	28	Saints/49ers	1981–1995
3.	Jason Taylor	27	Dolphins/Redskins/Jets	1997–2011
4.	Cornelius Bennett	26	Bills/Falcons/Colts	1987–2000
	Kevin Greene	26	Rams/Steelers/Panthers/49ers	1985–1999
6.	Dick Butkus	25	Bears	1965–1973

SINGLE SEASON

1.	Don Hultz	9	Vikings	1963
2.	Joe Schmidt	8	Lions	1955
3.	Ray Childress	7	Oilers	1988
	Rickey Jackson	7	Saints	1990
	Jack Lambert	7	Steelers	1976
	Alan Page	7	Vikings	1970

▲ Jack Lambert

WRONG-WAY MARSHALL

While no official records are kept for the longest safety, it would be hard to top one by Jim Marshall. The Vikings' defensive lineman was known for picking up fumbles and running with the ball. He grabbed one in a game against the 49ers in 1964. He sprinted 66 yards for what he thought was a touchdown. He flipped the ball into the air to celebrate the score, but he quickly realized his error. His run ended up being two points for the Niners instead of six for the Vikings. Marshall ran the wrong way, but the Vikings held on to win 27-22.

DEFENSIVE FUMBLE RECOVERIES

▼ Ronde Barber

CAREER FUMBLE RETURNS FOR TOUCHDOWNS ||||||||||

1.	Jason Taylor	6	Dolphins/Redskins/Jets	1997–2011
2.	Jessie Tuggle	5	Falcons	1987–2000
3.	Ronde Barber	4	Buccaneers	1997–2011*
	Keith Bulluck	4	Titans/Giants	2000–2010
	Derrick Thomas	4	Chiefs	1989–1999
	Bill Thompson	4	Broncos	1969–1981

*active player

SACKS

CAREER ||||||||||||||||||||||||||||||||||||||||||

1.	Bruce Smith	200	Bills/Redskins	1985–2003
2.	Reggie White	198	Eagles/Packers/Panthers	1985–2000
3.	Kevin Greene	160	Rams/Steelers/Panthers/49ers	1985–1999
4.	Chris Doleman	150½	Vikings/Falcons/49ers	1985–1999
5.	Michael Strahan	141½	Giants	1993–2007
6.	Jason Taylor	139½	Dolphins/Redskins/Jets	1997–2011
7.	Richard Dent	137½	Bears/49ers/Colts/Eagles	1983–1997
	John Randle	137½	Vikings/Seahawks	1990–2003
9.	Leslie O'Neal	132½	Chargers/Rams/Chiefs	1986–1999
	Lawrence Taylor	132½	Giants	1981–1993

▲ Reggie White

RECORD FACT Deacon Jones was one of the most ferocious pass rushers in NFL history. He played for the Los Angeles Rams, San Diego Chargers, and Washington Redskins from 1961 to 1974. He became known for bringing down quarterbacks. Jones helped come up with the term "sack." But he doesn't show up in the record books because the statistic did not become official until 1982.

SINGLE SEASON				
1.	Michael Strahan	22½	Giants	2001
2.	Jared Allen	22	Vikings	2011
	Mark Gastineau	22	Jets	1984
4.	Chris Doleman	21	Vikings	1989
	Reggie White	21	Eagles	1987
6.	Lawrence Taylor	20½	Giants	1986
7.	Derrick Thomas	20	Chiefs	1990
	DeMarcus Ware	20	Cowboys	2008
9.	Tim Harris	19½	Packers	1989
	DeMarcus Ware	19½	Cowboys	2011

▲ Michael Strahan

SACK ATTACK

In 1990 Kansas City Chiefs linebacker Derrick Thomas set the single-game sack record. He tackled Seattle Seahawks quarterback Dave Krieg behind the line of scrimmage seven times. On the last play of the game, Thomas almost got Krieg an eighth time. The quarterback managed to get away and complete the game-winning touchdown pass.

▲ Derrick Thomas

PUNT RETURNS FOR TOUCHDOWNS

▼ Brian Mitchell

CAREER

1.	Devin Hester	12	Bears	2006–2011*
2.	Eric Metcalf	10	Browns/Falcons/ Chargers/Cardinals/ Panthers/Redskins/ Packers	1989–2002
3.	Brian Mitchell	9	Redskins/Eagles/ Giants	1990–2003
4.	Jack Christiansen	8	Lions	1951–1958
	Desmond Howard	8	Redskins/Jaguars/ Packers/Raiders/ Lions	1992–2002
	Rick Upchurch	8	Broncos	1975–1983
7.	Dave Meggett	7	Giants/Patriots/Jets	1989–1998
8.	Five players tied with	6		

*active player

SINGLE SEASON

1.	Jack Christiansen	4	Lions	1951
	Devin Hester	4	Bears	2007
	Patrick Peterson	4	Cardinals	2011
	Rick Upchurch	4	Broncos	1976
5.	Many players tied with	3		

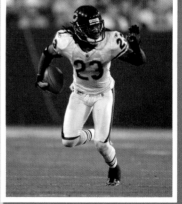

▲ Devin Hester

RECORD FACT The Arizona Cardinals' Patrick Peterson didn't wait long to burst into the record books. He returned four punts for touchdowns in 2011, tying the single-season record in his first NFL season.

KICKOFF RETURNS FOR TOUCHDOWNS

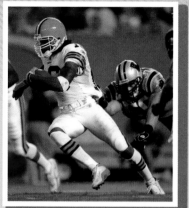

CARETR

1.	Josh Cribbs	8	Browns	2005–2011*
2.	Leon Washington	7	Jets/Seahawks	2006–2011*
3.	Mel Gray	6	Saints/Lions/ Oilers/Titans/ Eagles	1986–1997
	Dante Hall	6	Chiefs/Rams	2000–2008
	Ollie Matson	6	Cardinals/Rams/ Lions/Eagles	1952–1966
	Gale Sayers	6	Bears	1965–1971
	Travis Williams	6	Packers/Rams	1967–1971
8.	Many players tied with	5		

*active player

SINGLE SEASON

1.	Cecil Turner	4	Bears	1970
	Travis Williams	4	Packers	1967
3.	Many players tied with	3		

RECORD FACT Some teams never learn that you shouldn't kick to Devin Hester—no matter the situation. The record for most combined kick and punt returns for touchdowns belongs to the Bears' superstar. Besides his record 12 punt returns for scores, he also has taken five kickoffs all the way. In Super Bowl XLI, Hester took the game's opening kickoff 92 yards for a touchdown.

GAMES PLAYED |||||||||||||||||||||||||||||||||||||||||

1.	Morten Andersen, K	382	Saints/Falcons/Giants/Chiefs/Vikings	1982–2007
2.	Gary Anderson, K	353	Steelers/Eagles/49ers/Vikings/Titans	1982–2004
3.	Jeff Feagles, P	352	Patriots/Eagles/Cardinals/Seahawks/Giants	1988–2009
4.	George Blanda, QB/K	340	Bears/Colts/Oilers/Raiders	1949–1975
5.	Jason Hanson, K	312	Lions	1992–2011*
6.	Jerry Rice, WR	303	49ers/Raiders/Seahawks	1985–2004
7.	John Carney, K	302	Buccaneers/Rams/Chargers/Saints/Jaguars/Chiefs/Giants	1988–2010
	Brett Favre, QB	302	Falcons/Packers/Jets/Vikings	1988–2010
	John Kasay, K	302	Seahawks/Panthers/Saints	1991–2011*
10.	Matt Stover, K	297	Browns/Ravens/Colts	1991–2009

*active player

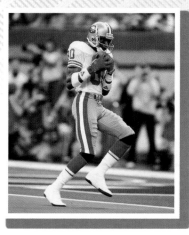

▲ Jerry Rice

IRONMEN

Two of the greatest records in sports involve playing streaks. In pro baseball Baltimore Orioles great Cal Ripken Jr. played 2,632 consecutive games over 17 seasons. In pro football Brett Favre started 297 straight games at quarterback over 19 seasons. Which player is the true Ironman? Baseball has 162 games in a season, while football has just 16. But football players get hit and tackled every game.

CONSECUTIVE GAMES STARTED

1.	Brett Favre, QB	297 (321 with playoff games)	Packers/Jets/Vikings	1992–2010
2.	Jim Marshall, DE	270 (289)	Vikings	1961–1979
3.	Mick Tingelhoff, C	240 (259)	Vikings	1962–1978
4.	Bruce Matthews, OL	229 (244)	Oilers/Titans	1987–2002
5.	Will Shields, OG	223 (231)	Chiefs	1993–2006
6.	Alan Page, DT	215 (234)	Vikings/Bears	1967–1981
7.	Jim Otto, C	210 (223)	Raiders	1960–1974
8.	Derrick Brooks, LB	208 (219)	Buccaneers	1996–2008
	Peyton Manning, QB	208 (227)	Colts	1998–2010
10.	Gene Upshaw, OG	207 (231)	Raiders	1967–1981

CONSECUTIVE GAMES PLAYED

1.	Jeff Feagles, P	352 (363)	Patriots/Eagles/ Cardinals/ Seahawks/Giants	1988– 2009
2.	Brett Favre, QB	299 (323)	Packers/Jets/Vikings	1992– 2010
3.	Jim Marshall, DE	282 (301)	Browns/Vikings	1960– 1979
4.	Morten Andersen, K	248 (256)	Saints/Falcons/ Giants/Chiefs	1987– 2002
5.	Chris Gardocki, P	244 (258)	Bears/Colts/Browns/ Steelers	1991– 2006
6.	Bill Romanowski, LB	243 (271)	49ers/Eagles/ Broncos/Raiders	1988– 2003
7.	Ryan Longwell, K	240 (253)	Packers/Vikings	1997– 2011*
	Mick Tingelhoff, C	240 (259)	Vikings	1962– 1978
9.	Gary Anderson, K	234 (251)	Steelers/Eagles/ 49ers/Vikings	1987– 2002
	Jim Bakken, K	234 (236)	Cardinals	1962– 1978

▲ Jeff Feagles

*active player

ALL-PURPOSE YARDS
(RUSHING, RECEIVING, RETURNING)

▼ Marshall Faulk

CAREER ||||||||||||||||||||||||||||||||||||||||||

1.	Jerry Rice	23,546	49ers/Raiders/Seahawks	1985–2004
2.	Brian Mitchell	23,316	Redskins/Eagles/Giants	1990–2003
3.	Walter Payton	21,803	Bears	1975–1987
4.	Emmitt Smith	21,579	Cowboys/Cardinals	1990–2004
5.	Tim Brown	19,679	Raiders/Buccaneers	1988–2004
6.	Marshall Faulk	19,172	Colts/Rams	1994–2005
7.	LaDainian Tomlinson	18,456	Chargers/Jets	2001–2011*
8.	Barry Sanders	18,308	Lions	1989–1998
9.	Herschel Walker	18,168	Cowboys/Vikings/Eagles/Giants	1986–1997
10.	Marcus Allen	17,654	Raiders/Chiefs	1982–1997

*active player

SINGLE SEASON ||||||||||||||||||||||||||||||||||||||

1.	Darren Sproles	2,696	Saints	2011
2.	Derrick Mason	2,690	Titans	2000
3.	Michael Lewis	2,647	Saints	2002
4.	Lionel James	2,535	Chargers	1985
5.	Fred Jackson	2,516	Bills	2009
6.	Josh Cribbs	2,510	Browns	2009
7.	Chris Johnson	2,509	Titans	2009
8.	Brian Mitchell	2,477	Redskins	1994
9.	Dante Hall	2,446	Chiefs	2003
10.	Mack Herron	2,444	Patriots	1974

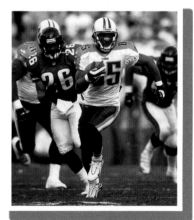

▼ Derrick Mason

CHAMPION COACHES

▼ Chuck Noll

Two coaches share the record for most championships won. The Bears' George Halas and the Packers' Curly Lambeau each won six NFL titles before the Super Bowl era began. Halas won in 1921, 1933, 1940, 1941, 1946, and 1963. Lambeau won in 1929, 1930, 1931, 1936, 1939, and 1944. Next on the list is the Packers' Vince Lombardi. His teams won five titles, including the first two Super Bowls. The Super Bowl trophy is named for Lombardi. The coach with the most Super Bowl wins is the Steelers' Chuck Noll, who won four Lombardi Trophies in the 1970s.

COACHING WINS ||||||||||||||||||||||||||||||||||||||||||||

1.	Don Shula	328	Colts/Dolphins	1963–1995
2.	George Halas	318	Staleys/Bears	1920–1967
3.	Tom Landry	250	Cowboys	1960–1988
4.	Curly Lambeau	226	Packers/ Cardinals/ Redskins	1921–1953
5.	Paul Brown	213	Browns/ Bengals	1946–1975
6.	Marty Schottenheimer	200	Browns/Chiefs/ Redskins/ Chargers	1984–2006
7.	Chuck Noll	193	Steelers	1969–1991
8.	Dan Reeves	190	Broncos/Giants/ Falcons	1981–2003
9.	Chuck Knox	186	Rams/Bills/ Seahawks	1973–1994
10.	Bill Belichick	175	Browns/Patriots	1991–2011*

*active coach

▲ Tom Landry

CHAPTER 2

TEAM RECORDS

Many consider football the ultimate team game. Each player on the field has a job to do, whether it's blocking, tackling, throwing, catching, or running. If it's all done well together, a team will have success, put points on the board, and win games. The team can also set records. The best teams hold records for the most championships, the most wins, and the most points.

Can you imagine what it would have been like to watch the 1940 NFL championship game? The Chicago Bears played the Washington Redskins and beat them 73-0! No team has scored more points in a single game than the Bears did that day. And you thought the New England Patriots, who scored 589 points in 2007, were good! Check out some of the best team records in NFL history.

▲ **New England Patriots**

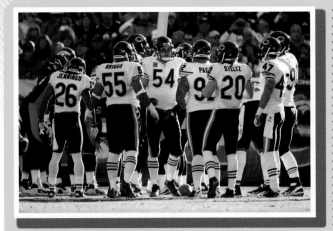

▲ Chicago Bears

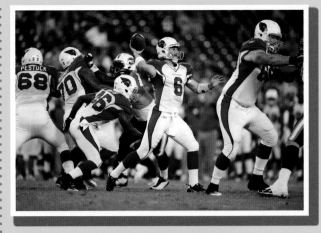

▲ Arizona Cardinals

WINS (NFL 1920–2011)		
1.	Bears	712
2.	Packers	679
3.	Giants	645
4.	Steelers	553
5.	Redskins	552
6.	49ers	522
7.	Eagles	517
8.	Rams	513
9.	Lions	506
10.	Cardinals	496

LOSSES (NFL 1920–2011)		
1.	Cardinals	699
2.	Lions	599
3.	Eagles	549
4.	Giants	531
5.	Redskins	527
6.	Packers	525
7.	Bears	520
8.	Rams	506
9.	Steelers	503
10.	49ers	423

MOST POINTS IN A SEASON			
1.	Patriots	589	2007
2.	Packers	560	2011
3.	Vikings	556	1998
4.	Saints	547	2011
5.	Redskins	541	1983
6.	Rams	540	2000
7.	Rams	526	1999
8.	Colts	522	2004
9.	Patriots	518	2010
10.	Dolphins	513	1984
	Patriots	513	2011

 Wide receiver Randy Moss played for two of the three highest-scoring teams of all time. He was a rookie with the 1998 Vikings and later played for the 2007 Patriots. Both teams made the playoffs, but the Vikings lost in the NFC championship, and the Patriots lost in the Super Bowl.

▼ Washington Redskins

MOST TEAM POINTS IN A GAME ||||||||||||||||||||||||||

1.	Redskins	72	Nov. 27, 1966	vs. Giants
2.	Rams	70	Oct. 22, 1950	vs. Colts
3.	Browns	66	Dec. 8, 1946	vs. Dodgers
	Jeffersons	66	Oct. 10, 1920	vs. Fort Porter
5.	Cardinals	65	Nov. 13, 1949	vs. Bulldogs
	Rams	65	Oct. 29, 1950	vs. Lions
7.	49ers	63	Nov. 21, 1948	vs. Dodgers
	Cardinals	63	Oct. 17, 1948	vs. Giants
	Steelers	63	Nov. 30, 1952	vs. Giants
10.	Six teams tied with	62		

MOST TOTAL POINTS IN A GAME ||||||||||||||||||||||||||||

1.	Redskins 72, Giants 41	113	Nov. 27, 1966
2.	Bengals 58, Browns 48	106	Nov. 28, 2004
3.	49ers 63, Dodgers 40	103	Nov. 21, 1948
4.	Raiders 52, Oilers 49	101	Dec. 22, 1963
5.	Seahawks 51, Chiefs 48 (OT)	99	Nov. 27, 1983

▲ Cincinnati Bengals

 **RECORD FACT** The Buccaneers were an expansion team in 1976. They lost all 14 games of their first season and 12 games to start the following season. The 2008 Lions are the only team to lose every game of a 16-game season.

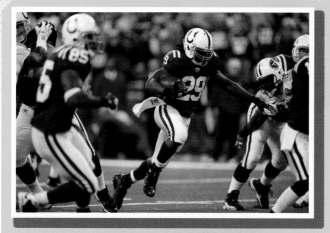

▲ Indianapolis Colts

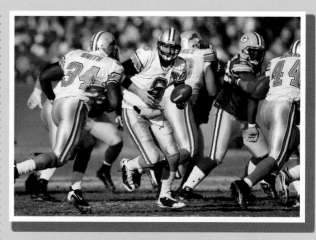

▲ Detroit Lions

CONSECUTIVE WINS |||||||||||||||||| (REGULAR SEASON)

1.	Colts	23	2008–2009
2.	Patriots	21	2006–2008
3.	Patriots	18	2003–2004
4.	Bears	17	1933–1934
5.	Bears	16	1941–1942
	Dolphins	16	1983–1984
	Dolphins	16	1971–1973
	Steelers	16	2004–2005

CONSECUTIVE LOSSES |||||||||||||| (REGULAR SEASON)

1.	Buccaneers	26	1976–1977
2.	Cardinals	19	1942–1943, 1945
	Lions	19	2007–2009
	Raiders	19	1961–1962
5.	Oilers	18	1972–1973

BIG WINNERS

The 2007 New England Patriots won all 16 games of the regular season. They advanced to the Super Bowl, where they were shocked by the New York Giants. The 1972 Dolphins remain the only team to win every game of the regular season (14 at the time) and go on to win the Super Bowl.

▲ The Giants defense swarms Patriots' quarterback Tom Brady during Super Bowl XLII.

CHAPTER 3

POSTSEASON RECORDS

Every team in the NFL starts the season with the goal of making the playoffs. The ultimate prize is playing in the Super Bowl and winning a championship. The postseason has featured many outstanding and memorable performances. Some of the performances have put players and teams into the record books.

In 1995 Steve Young, the 49ers quarterback, broke a record set by another 49ers quarterback, Joe Montana. Young threw six touchdown passes against the San Diego Chargers in Super Bowl XXIX. Montana had tossed five touchdowns against the Denver Broncos five years earlier.

Who can forget the January 10, 2010, playoff shootout between Kurt Warner's Arizona Cardinals and Aaron Rodgers' Green Bay Packers? The high-powered offenses combined for the highest-scoring playoff game of all time. The Cardinals won the game 51-45 on a defensive touchdown in overtime.

▲ Steve Young

SUPER BOWL

PASSING TOUCHDOWNS ||||||||||||||||||||||||||||||||||

1.	Steve Young	6	49ers	Super Bowl XXIX
2.	Joe Montana	5	49ers	Super Bowl XXIV
3.	Troy Aikman	4	Cowboys	Super Bowl XXVII
	Terry Bradshaw	4	Steelers	Super Bowl XIII
	Doug Williams	4	Redskins	Super Bowl XXII
6.	Many players tied with	3		

PASSING YARDS ||||||||||||||||||||||||||||||||||

1.	Kurt Warner	414	Rams	Super Bowl XXXIV
2.	Kurt Warner	377	Cardinals	Super Bowl XLIII
3.	Kurt Warner	365	Rams	Super Bowl XXXVI
4.	Donovan McNabb	357	Eagles	Super Bowl XXXIX
	Joe Montana	357	49ers	Super Bowl XXIII
6.	Tom Brady	354	Patriots	Super Bowl XXXVIII
7.	Doug Williams	340	Redskins	Super Bowl XXII
8.	John Elway	336	Broncos	Super Bowl XXXIII
9.	Peyton Manning	333	Colts	Super Bowl XLIV
10.	Joe Montana	331	49ers	Super Bowl XIX

▲ Kurt Warner

ROMAN NUMERAL GUIDE

1.	I	5.	V	9.	IX	13.	XIII	17.	XVII	30.	XXX
2.	II	6.	VI	10.	X	14.	XIV	18.	XVIII	40.	XL
3.	III	7.	VII	11.	XI	15.	XV	19.	XIX	50.	L
4.	IV	8.	VIII	12.	XII	16.	XVI	20.	XX		

SUPER BOWL

PASSES COMPLETED

1.	Tom Brady	32	Patriots	Super Bowl XXXVIII
	Drew Brees	32	Saints	Super Bowl XLIV
3.	Jim Kelly	31	Bills	Super Bowl XXXVIII
	Peyton Manning	31	Colts	Super Bowl XLIV
	Kurt Warner	31	Cardinals	Super Bowl XLIII
6.	Donovan McNabb	30	Eagles	Super Bowl XXXIX
7.	Tom Brady	29	Patriots	Super Bowl XLII
	Dan Marino	29	Dolphins	Super Bowl XIX
9.	Jim Kelly	28	Bills	Super Bowl XXVI
	Neil O'Donnell	28	Steelers	Super Bowl XXX
	Kurt Warner	28	Rams	Super Bowl XXXVI

LONGEST PASS (ALL TOUCHDOWNS)

1.	Jake Delhomme to Muhsin Muhammad	85 yards	Panthers	Super Bowl XXXVIII
2.	Brett Favre to Antonio Freeman	81 yards	Packers	Super Bowl XXXI
3.	John Elway to Rod Smith	80 yards	Broncos	Super Bowl XXXIII
	Jim Plunkett to Kenny King	80 yards	Raiders	Super Bowl XV
	Doug Williams to Ricky Sanders	80 yards	Redskins	Super Bowl XXII
6.	David Woodley to Jimmy Cefalo	76 yards	Dolphins	Super Bowl XVII
7.	Terry Bradshaw to John Stallworth	75 yards	Steelers	Super Bowl XIII
	Johnny Unitas to John Mackey	75 yards	Colts	Super Bowl V
9.	Terry Bradshaw to John Stallworth	73 yards	Steelers	Super Bowl XIV
	Kurt Warner to Isaac Bruce	73 yards	Rams	Super Bowl XXXIV

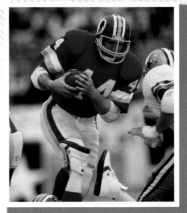

▼ John Riggins

RUSHING YARDS

1.	Timmy Smith	204	Redskins	Super Bowl XXII
2.	Marcus Allen	191	Raiders	Super Bowl XVIII
3.	John Riggins	166	Redskins	Super Bowl XVII
4.	Franco Harris	158	Steelers	Super Bowl IX
5.	Terrell Davis	157	Broncos	Super Bowl XXXII
6.	Larry Csonka	145	Dolphins	Super Bowl VIII
7.	Clarence Davis	137	Raiders	Super Bowl XI
8.	Thurman Thomas	135	Bills	Super Bowl XXV
9.	Emmitt Smith	132	Cowboys	Super Bowl XXVIII
10.	Michael Pittman	124	Buccaneers	Super Bowl XXXVII

LONGEST RUN

1.	Willie Parker	75 yards (TD)	Steelers	Super Bowl XL
2.	Marcus Allen	74 yards (TD)	Raiders	Super Bowl XVIII
3.	Tom Matte	58 yards	Colts	Super Bowl III
	Timmy Smith	58 yards (TD)	Redskins	Super Bowl XXII
5.	Thomas Jones	52 yards	Bears	Super Bowl XLI
6.	Larry Csonka	49 yards	Dolphins	Super Bowl VII
7.	Alvin Garrett	44 yards	Redskins	Super Bowl XVII
8.	John Riggins	43 yards (TD)	Redskins	Super Bowl XVII
	Timmy Smith	43 yards	Redskins	Super Bowl XXII
10.	Marcus Allen	39 yards	Raiders	Super Bowl XVIII
	Wendell Tyler	39 yards	Rams	Super Bowl XIV

▲ Willie Parker

SUPER BOWL

RECEPTIONS ||||||||||||||||||||||||||||||

1.	Deion Branch	11	Patriots	Super Bowl XXXIX
	Jerry Rice	11	49ers	Super Bowl XXIII
	Dan Ross	11	Bengals	Super Bowl XVI
	Wes Welker	11	Patriots	Super Bowl XLII
5.	Joseph Addai	10	Colts	Super Bowl XLI
	Deion Branch	10	Patriots	Super Bowl XXXVIII
	Andre Hastings	10	Steelers	Super Bowl XXX
	Tony Nathan	10	Dolphins	Super Bowl XIX
	Hakeem Nicks	10	Giants	Super Bowl XLVI
	Jerry Rice	10	49ers	Super Bowl XXIX

RECEIVING YARDS ||||||||||||||||||||||||||

1.	Jerry Rice	215	49ers	Super Bowl XXIII
2.	Ricky Sanders	193	Redskins	Super Bowl XXII
3.	Isaac Bruce	162	Rams	Super Bowl XXXIV
4.	Lynn Swann	161	Steelers	Super Bowl X
5.	Andre Reed	152	Bills	Super Bowl XXVII
	Rod Smith	152	Broncos	Super Bowl XXXIII
7.	Jerry Rice	149	49ers	Super Bowl XXIX
8.	Jerry Rice	148	49ers	Super Bowl XXIV
9.	Deion Branch	143	Patriots	Super Bowl XXXVIII
10.	Muhsin Muhammad	140	Panthers	Super Bowl XXXVIII
	Jordy Nelson	140	Packers	Super Bowl XLV

▲ Lynn Swann

RECORD FACT

In 1995 San Francisco 49ers receiver Jerry Rice tied the record for receiving touchdowns during a Super Bowl with three. Who did he tie? Himself! He achieved the feat five years earlier during Super Bowl XXIV.

The Oakland Raiders' Rod Martin is the only player to grab three interceptions in a Super Bowl. He picked off three passes against the Philadelphia Eagles in Super Bowl XV. Eleven players have had two interceptions. Only the Tampa Bay Buccaneers' Dwight Smith took both picks back for touchdowns.

Two players have had three sacks in a Super Bowl: the Packers' Reggie White and the Cardinals' Darnell Dockett.

Three players have had two defensive fumble recoveries in a Super Bowl: the Dallas Cowboys' Randy Hughes, the Chicago Bears' Mike Singletary, and the Dallas Cowboys' Jimmie Jones. There have been five defensive fumble recoveries for touchdowns in Super Bowl history.

The longest interception return for a touchdown in a Super Bowl game was 100 yards. Pittsburgh Steelers linebacker James Harrison did it against the Cardinals in Super Bowl XLIII.

RECORD FACT Mike Lodish of the Buffalo Bills and the Denver Broncos appeared in six Super Bowls, more than any other player. Fourteen players have played in five games. Only one, Charles Haley of the San Francisco 49ers and Dallas Cowboys, has won five Super Bowl rings. Don Shula coached the Baltimore Colts and Miami Dolphins to six Super Bowls, more than any other coach.

SUPER BOWL

▲ 49ers vs. Broncos

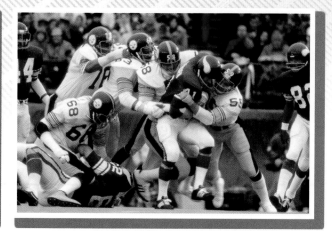

▲ Vikings vs. Steelers

MOST POINTS IN A SUPER BOWL ||||||

1.	49ers	55	Super Bowl XXIV vs. Broncos
2.	Cowboys	52	Super Bowl XXVII vs. Bills
3.	49ers	49	Super Bowl XXIX vs. Chargers
4.	Buccaneers	48	Super Bowl XXXVII vs. Raiders
5.	Bears	46	Super Bowl XX vs. Patriots
6.	Redskins	42	Super Bowl XXII vs. Broncos
7.	Giants	39	Super Bowl XXI vs. Broncos
8.	49ers	38	Super Bowl XIX vs. Dolphins
	Raiders	38	Super Bowl XVIII vs. Redskins
10.	Redskins	37	Super Bowl XXVI vs. Bills

FEWEST POINTS IN A SUPER BOWL ||||

1.	Dolphins	3	Super Bowl VI vs. Cowboys
2.	Vikings	6	Super Bowl IX vs. Steelers
3.	Colts	7	Super Bowl III vs. Jets
	Giants	7	Super Bowl XXXV vs. Ravens
	Redskins	7	Super Bowl VII vs. Dolphins
	Vikings	7	Super Bowl IV vs. Chiefs
	Vikings	7	Super Bowl VIII vs. Dolphins
8.	Redskins	9	Super Bowl XVIII vs. Raiders
9.	Many teams tied with	10	

SUPER BOWL

▼ **49ers vs. Chargers**

MOST TOTAL POINTS IN A SUPER BOWL ||||||||||||||

1.	49ers 49, Chargers 26	75	Super Bowl XXIX
2.	Buccaneers 48, Raiders 21	69	Super Bowl XXXVII
	Cowboys 52, Bills 17	69	Super Bowl XXVII
4.	Steelers 35, Cowboys 31	66	Super Bowl XIII
5.	49ers 55, Broncos 10	65	Super Bowl XXIV
6.	Patriots 32, Panthers 29	61	Super Bowl XXXVIII
	Redskins 37, Bills 24	61	Super Bowl XXVI
8.	Giants 39, Broncos 20	59	Super Bowl XXI
9.	Bears 46, Patriots 10	56	Super Bowl XX
	Packers 35, Patriots 21	56	Super Bowl XXXI
	Packers 31, Steelers 25	56	Super Bowl XLV

FEWEST POINTS IN A SUPER BOWL |||||||||||||||||||

1.	Dolphins 14, Redskins 7	21	Super Bowl VII
2.	Steelers 16, Vikings 6	22	Super Bowl IX
3.	Jets 16, Colts 7	23	Super Bowl III
4.	Cowboys 24, Dolphins 3	27	Super Bowl VI
5.	Colts 16, Cowboys 13	29	Super Bowl V
6.	Chiefs 23, Vikings 7	30	Super Bowl IV
7.	Dolphins 24, Vikings 7	31	Super Bowl VIII
	Giants 17, Patriots 14	31	Super Bowl XLII
	Steelers 21, Seahawks 10	31	Super Bowl XL
10.	49ers 20, Bengals 16	36	Super Bowl XXIII

▲ **Steelers vs. Seahawks**

RECORD FACT The longest fumble return in Super Bowl history belongs to the Dallas Cowboys' Leon Lett. During Super Bowl XXVII, the defensive lineman went 64 yards and should have scored a touchdown. But he celebrated early with the ball out. The Buffalo Bills' Don Beebe chased him down and knocked the ball out of his hand. The ball went out the side of the end zone for a touchback. Luckily for Lett, the Cowboys won the game.

CHARPIONSHIPS ||||||||

1.	Packers	13
2.	Bears	9
3.	Browns	8
	Giants	8
5.	Steelers	6
6.	49ers	5
	Cowboys	5
	Redskins	5
9.	Colts	4
	Lions	4

▲ Green Bay Packers

THE START OF THE BOWL

The Super Bowl era started after the 1966 season. The champions of the National Football League and the American Football League played each other. Super Bowl I featured the Green Bay Packers of the NFL and the Kansas City Chiefs of the AFL. The Packers won the game 35-10. Eventually the two leagues merged into one. Each year teams play to become Super Bowl champs and winners of the Lombardi Trophy.

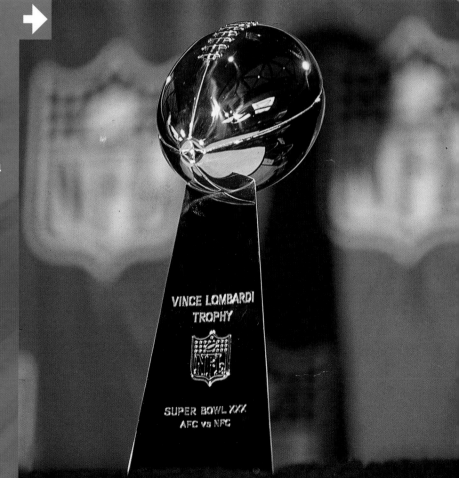

SUPER BOWL

▲ Pittsburgh Steelers

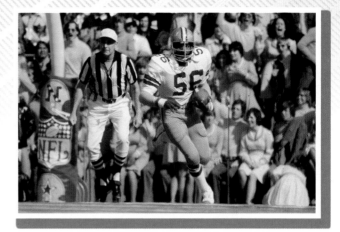

▲ Dallas Cowboys

SUPER BOWL WINS ||||||||||||||||||

1.	Steelers	6
2.	49ers	5
	Cowboys	5
4.	Giants	4
	Packers	4
6.	Patriots	3
	Raiders	3
	Redskins	3
9.	Broncos	2
	Colts	2
	Dolphins	2

SUPER BOWL APPEARANCES ||||||||||

1.	Cowboys	8
	Steelers	8
3.	Patriots	7
4.	Broncos	6
5.	49ers	5
	Dolphins	5
	Giants	5
	Packers	5
	Raiders	5
	Redskins	5

IN THE SPOTLIGHT

Three teams have lost the Super Bowl four times. Two of them—the Vikings and Bills—have never won a title. The Broncos lost their first four Super Bowl games before winning back-to-back championships following the 1997 and 1998 seasons. The only team to appear in more than one Super Bowl and never lose is the 49ers. The team is 5-0 in title games.

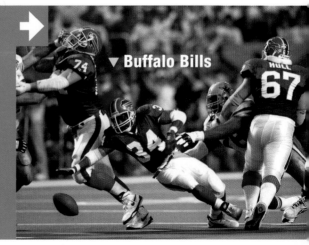

▼ Buffalo Bills

PLAYOFFS

PLAYOFF APPEARANCES ||||||||||

1.	Cowboys	30
	Giants	30
3.	Browns	28
4.	Rams	27
5.	Packers	26
	Steelers	26
	Vikings	26
8.	Bears	25
9.	Colts	24
10.	Eagles	23

MOST POINTS IN A PLAYOFF GAME |||||||||||||

1.	Bears	73	1940	vs. Redskins
2.	Jaguars	62	1999	vs. Dolphins
3.	Lions	59	1957	vs. Browns
4.	Eagles	58	1995	vs. Lions
5.	Browns	56	1954	vs. Lions
	Raiders	56	1969	vs. Oilers
7.	49ers	55	1990	vs. Broncos
8.	Cowboys	52	1967	vs. Browns
	Cowboys	52	1993	vs. Bills
10.	Four teams tied with	51		

MOST TOTAL POINTS IN A PLAYOFF GAME ||||||||

1.	Cardinals 51, Packers 45	96	2010
2.	Eagles 58, Lions 37	95	1995
3.	Rams 49, Vikings 37	86	2000

▲ Cardinals vs. Packers

 **PLAYOFFS**

▼ **Drew Brees**

PASSES COMPLETED IN A SINGLE PLAYOFF GAME

1.	Drew Brees	39	Saints	Jan. 8, 2011
2.	Warren Moon	36	Oilers	Jan. 3, 1993
3.	Dan Fouts	33	Chargers	Jan. 2, 1982
	Bernie Kosar	33	Browns	Jan. 3, 1987
	Peyton Manning	33	Colts	Jan. 13, 2008
	Dan Marino	33	Dolphins	Dec. 30, 1985
7.	Several players tied at	32		

PASSING YARDS IN A SINGLE PLAYOFF GAME

1.	Bernie Kosar	489	Browns	Jan. 3, 1987
2.	Peyton Manning	458	Colts	Jan. 9, 2005
3.	Dan Fouts	433	Chargers	Jan. 2, 1982

LONGEST PASS

1.	Trent Dilfer to Shannon Sharpe	96 yards (TD)	Ravens	Jan. 14, 2001
2.	Troy Aikman to Alvin Harper	94 yards (TD)	Cowboys	Jan. 8, 1995
3.	Daryle Lamonica to Elbert Dubenion	93 yards (TD)	Bills	Dec. 28, 1963

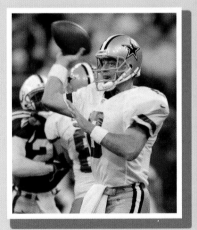

▲ **Troy Aikman**

 **RECORD FACT** Trent Dilfer's record-breaking touchdown pass to Shannon Sharpe was only one of nine passes he completed that game. It was the only touchdown of the game, with the Ravens beating the Raiders 16-3.

▼ **Kurt Warner**

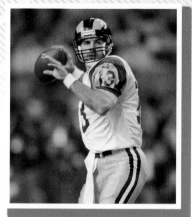

TOUCHDOWN PASSES IN A SINGLE PLAYOFF GAME

1.	Daryle Lamonica	6	Raiders	Dec. 21, 1969
	Steve Young	6	49ers	Jan. 29, 1995
3.	Kerry Collins	5	Giants	Jan. 14, 2001
	Daryle Lamonica	5	Raiders	Dec. 22, 1968
	Sid Luckman	5	Bears	Dec. 26, 1943
	Peyton Manning	5	Colts	Jan. 4, 2004
	Joe Montana	5	49ers	Jan. 28, 1990
	Kurt Warner	5	Rams	Jan. 16, 2000
	Kurt Warner	5	Cardinals	Jan. 10, 2010
10.	Many players tied with	4		

INTERCEPTIONS THROWN IN A SINGLE PLAYOFF GAME

1.	Brett Favre	6	Packers	Jan. 20, 2002
	Frank Filchock	6	Giants	Dec. 15, 1946
	Bobby Layne	6	Lions	Dec. 26, 1954
	Norm Van Brocklin	6	Rams	Dec. 26, 1955
5.	Many players tied with	5		

▲ **Bobby Layne**

RECORD FACT The longest field goal in playoff history was 58 yards. The booming kick came from the Dolphins' Pete Stoyanovich during the 1990 AFC playoff victory against the Chiefs.

PLAYOFFS

RUSHING YARDS IN A SINGLE GAME |||||||||||||||||||

1.	Eric Dickerson	248	Rams	Jan. 4, 1986
2.	Lamar Smith	209	Dolphins	Dec. 30, 2000
3.	Keith Lincoln	206	Chargers	Jan. 5, 1964

LONGEST RUN |||||||||||||||||||||||||||||||

1.	Fred Taylor	90 yards (TD)	Jaguars	Jan. 15, 2000
2.	Ray Rice	83 yards (TD)	Ravens	Jan. 10, 2010
3.	Roger Craig	80 yards (TD)	49ers	Jan. 1, 1989
	Charlie Garner	80 yards (TD)	Raiders	Jan. 12, 2002

▲ **Ray Rice**

RECORD FACT In 1993, 49ers running back Ricky Watters scored five touchdowns in a playoff game against the Giants.

KICKING WHEN IT COUNTS

Adam Vinatieri is one of the best clutch kickers to play in the NFL. He is the first kicker to win four Super Bowl rings. In two of those championships, he kicked the game-winning field goal in the closing seconds of the game. No kicker has made more playoff kicks than Vinatieri. He has booted 42 field goals in 23 playoff games over his career.

▼ Steve Smith

RECEPTIONS IN A SINGLE PLAYOFF GAME ||||||||||||

1.	Chad Morton	13	Saints	Jan. 6, 2001
	Shannon Sharpe	13	Broncos	Jan. 9, 1994
	Thurman Thomas	13	Bills	Jan. 6, 1990
	Kellen Winslow	13	Chargers	Jan. 2, 1982
5.	Raymond Berry	12	Colts	Dec. 28, 1958
	Michael Irvin	12	Cowboys	Jan. 15, 1995
	Darrell Jackson	12	Seahawks	Jan. 8, 2005
	Steve Smith	12	Panthers	Jan. 15, 2006
9.	Many players tied with	11		

RECEIVING YARDS IN A SINGLE PLAYOFF GAME ||||||||

1.	Eric Moulds	240	Bills	Jan. 2, 1999
2.	Anthony Carter	227	Vikings	Jan. 9, 1988
3.	Reggie Wayne	221	Colts	Jan. 9, 2005

▲ Reggie Wayne

RECORD FACTS Jerry Rice has caught three touchdown passes in a playoff game three times. Eleven other players have had three-touchdown playoff games, but Rice is the only player with more than one.

Seven kickers have made five field goals in a single playoff game. Adam Vinatieri did it twice, once as a New England Patriot and once as an Indianapolis Colt.

The Houston Oilers' Vernon Perry intercepted four passes against the Chargers during a playoff game in 1979. Seven players have had three-interception games.

The St. Louis Rams' Aeneas Williams and the Tampa Bay Buccaneers' **Dwight Smith** each have had two interceptions for touchdowns in the playoffs.

The Pittsburgh Steelers' Jack Lambert recovered three Oakland Raiders fumbles during a playoff game in 1975.

The New England Patriots' Willie McGinest made a record 4½ sacks against the Jaguars in a 2005 playoff game. The Washington Redskins' Rich Milot and the Chicago Bears' Richard Dent are next on the list with 3½ sacks.

WILD CARD WINNERS

Getting through the NFL playoffs and to the Super Bowl is a tough task for any team. The best four teams after the regular season get a bye for the first round of the playoffs. Teams that don't win their division but make the playoffs are called wild card teams. They have the toughest path to the big game, playing most of their games on the road. Only six wild card teams have worked their way through the playoffs to win the Lombardi Trophy. They were the Raiders (Super Bowl XV), the Broncos (XXXII), the Ravens (XXXV), the Steelers (XL), the Giants (XLII) and the Packers (XLV).

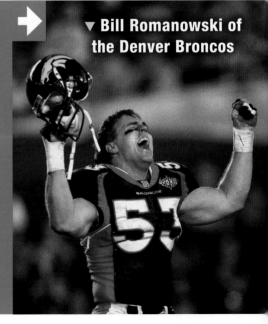

▼ Bill Romanowski of the Denver Broncos

CHAPTER 4

AROUND THE FIELD

▼ Brett Favre

There's an old saying that records were made to be broken. That might be true for some records, but some appear to be so out of reach that they'll stay on top forever.

When Brett Favre retired after the 2010 season, some thought the Colts' Peyton Manning could be on the way to approaching Favre's 297-game starting streak. But when an injury sidelined Manning before the 2011 season began, his streak ended at 208 games. The streak was good enough to come in second on the list, but it was 89 games behind Favre's run.

Will we ever see a team make a comeback like the Buffalo Bills in 1993? They were down by 32 points in a playoff game against the Houston Oilers. Down 35-3 in the third quarter, the Bills surged to a 41-38 overtime victory.

GREATEST COMEBACKS (REGULAR SEASON) ||||||||||||||||||||||||||||||||||

1.	**49ers 38, Saints 35**	49ers trailed by 28 (35-7)	Dec. 7, 1980
2.	**Bills 37, Colts 35**	Bills trailed by 26 (26-0)	Sept. 21, 1997
3.	**Cardinals 31, Buccaneers 28**	Cardinals trailed by 25 (28-3)	Nov. 8, 1987
4.	**Eagles 28, Redskins 24**	Eagles trailed by 24 (24-0)	Oct. 27, 1946
	Lions 31, Colts 27	Lions trailed by 24 (27-3)	Oct. 20, 1957
	Eagles 28, Cardinals 24	Eagles trailed by 24 (24-0)	Oct. 25, 1959
	Broncos 31, Patriots 24	Broncos trailed by 24 (24-0)	Oct. 23, 1960
	Dolphins 34, Patriots 27	Miami trailed by 24 (24-0)	Dec. 15, 1974
	Vikings 28, 49ers 27	Vikings trailed by 24 (24-0)	Dec. 4, 1977
	Broncos 37, Seahawks 34	Broncos trailed by 24 (34-10)	Sept. 23, 1979
	Oilers 30, Bengals 27	Oilers trailed by 24 (24-0)	Sept. 23, 1979
	Raiders 28, Chargers 24	Raiders trailed by 24 (24-0)	Nov. 22, 1982
	Raiders 30, Broncos 27	Raiders trailed by 24 (24-0)	Sept. 26, 1988
	Rams 31, Buccaneers 27	Rams trailed by 24 (27-3)	Dec. 6, 1992
	Lions 34, Cowboys 30	Lions trailed by 24 (27-3)	Oct. 2, 2011

GREATEST COMEBACKS (PLAYOFFS) |||||||||||||||||||||

1.	**Bills 41, Oilers 38**	Bills trailed by 32 (35-3)	Jan. 3, 1993
2.	**49ers 39, Giants 38**	49ers trailed by 24 (38-14)	Jan. 5, 2003
3.	**Lions 31, 49ers 27**	Lions trailed by 20 (27-7)	Dec. 22, 1957
4.	**Colts 38, Patriots 34**	Colts trailed by 18 (21-3)	Jan. 21, 2007
	Cowboys 30, 49ers 28	Cowboys trailed by 18 (21-3)	Dec. 23, 1972
	Dolphins 24, Browns 21	Dolphins trailed by 18 (21-3)	Jan. 4, 1986

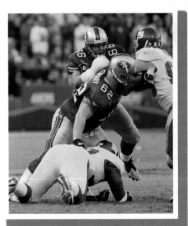

▲ **49ers vs. Giants**

Even though a football field is 100 yards without the end zones, there have been several plays that have topped the three-digit mark. Robert Bailey of the Los Angeles Rams returned a punt 103 yards for a touchdown October 23, 1994. Ellis Hobbs of the New England Patriots returned a kickoff 108 yards for a touchdown September 9, 2007. Randall Cobb of the Green Bay Packers did the same September 8, 2011. But the San Diego Chargers' Antonio Cromartie owns the longest play in NFL history. He returned a missed field goal 109 yards for a touchdown November 4, 2007.

▼ Ellis Hobbs

▲ Antonio Cromartie

▲ Randall Cobb

▼ Sammy Baugh

▼ In 1943 the Redskins' Sammy Baugh showed he could do it all. "Slingin' Sammy" led the NFL in passing on offense, interceptions on defense, and punting on special teams.

▼ The longest punt in NFL history went 98 yards. The New York Jets' Steve O'Neal booted the record-breaker September 21, 1969. He punted from the 1-yard line, and the ball rolled untouched to the opposite 1-yard line.

▼ Most interceptions thrown in a game: The Cardinals' Jim Hardy threw eight passes to the other team September 24, 1950.

▼ San Francisco 49ers

▼ Between 1988 and 1990, the San Francisco 49ers won 18 consecutive games on the road.

▼ Most yards passing in a game: The Rams' Norm Van Brocklin threw for 554 yards September 28, 1951.

▼ Johnny Unitas completed a touchdown pass in 47 consecutive games spanning four seasons. Drew Brees is sitting with 43, and he'll try for the record in the 2012 season.

COLDEST GAMES ||||||||||||||||||||||||||||||||||||||||||||||||||||||||||||||||||||||||||||||

1.	**Packers 21, Cowboys 17**	-13 degrees (wind chill -48)	Dec. 31, 1967	at Green Bay
2.	**Bengals 27, Chargers 7**	-9 degrees (wind chill -59)	Jan. 10, 1982	at Cincinnati
3.	**Colts 10, Chiefs 7**	-6 degrees	Jan. 7, 1996	at Kansas City
4.	**Raiders 14, Browns 12**	-5 degrees	Jan. 4, 1981	at Cleveland
5.	**Giants 23, Packers 20**	-4 degrees (wind chill -24)	Jan. 20, 2008	at Green Bay
6.	**Vikings 23, Bears 10**	-2 degrees (wind chill -26)	Dec. 3, 1972	at Minnesota
7.	**Packers 23, Vikings 7**	0 degrees (wind chill -18)	Dec. 10, 1972	at Minnesota
8.	**Packers 28, Raiders 0**	0 degrees	Dec. 26, 1993	at Green Bay
9.	**Bills 29, Raiders 23**	0 degrees (wind chill -32)	Jan. 15, 1994	at Buffalo
10.	**Lions 24, Packers 17**	2 degrees	Dec. 22, 1990	at Green Bay

*in degrees Fahrenheit

OLDEST TEAMS		
1.	Cardinals	1898 (started as the Morgan Athletic Club)
2.	Packers	1919 (oldest team still in the same city)
3.	Bears	1920 (started as the Decatur Staleys)
4.	Giants	1925
5.	Lions	1930
6.	Redskins	1932
7.	Eagles	1933
	Steelers	1933
9.	Rams	1937
10.	49ers	1946
	Browns	1946

▲ Chicago Bears

NEWEST TEAMS		
1.	Texans	2002
2.	Ravens	1996
3.	Jaguars	1995
	Panthers	1995
5.	Buccaneers	1976
	Seahawks	1976
7.	Bengals	1968
8.	Saints	1967
9.	Dolphins	1966
	Falcons	1966

▲ Jacksonville Jaguars

READ MORE

Berman, Len. *The Greatest Moments in Sports*. Naperville, Ill.: Sourcebooks, 2009.

Buckley Jr., James. *Super Bowl Fireworks*. New York: Scholastic, 2009.

Frederick, Shane. *The Best of Everything Football Book*. The All-Time Best of Sports. Mankato, Minn: Capstone Press, 2011.

Wiseman, Blaine. *Football*. Record Breakers. New York: AVA² by Weigl, 2011.

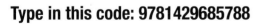

INTERNET SITES

FactHound offers a safe, fun way to find Internet sites related to this book. All of the sites on FactHound have been researched by our staff.

Here's all you do:

Visit *www.facthound.com*

Type in this code: 9781429685788

INDEX